I0110892

BUILDING BLOCKS OF ENGLISH

SENTENCES AND THEIR PARTS

Written by Jeff De La Rosa

Illustrated by Ruth Bennett

WORLD
BOOK

a Scott Fetzer company
Chicago

Co-published by agreement between Shi Tu Hui and World Book, Inc.

Shi Tu Hui
Room 1807, Block 1,
#3 West Dawang Road
Chaoyang District, Beijing 100025
P.R. China

World Book, Inc.
180 North LaSalle Street
Suite 900
Chicago, Illinois 60601
USA

WORLD BOOK STAFF

Editorial

Vice President
Tom Evans

Senior Manager, New Content
Jeff De La Rosa

Curriculum Designer
Caroline Davidson

Proofreader
Nathalie Strassheim

Graphics and Design

Senior Visual Communications Designer
Melanie Bender

Library of Congress Control Number: 2024936274

Building Blocks of English
ISBN: 978-0-7166-5517-6 (set, hardcover)

Sentences and Their Parts
ISBN: 978-0-7166-5523-7 (hardcover)

Also available as:
ISBN:978-0-7166-5533-6 (e-book)
ISBN: 978-0-7166-5543-5 (soft cover)

Acknowledgments:
Writer: Jeff De La Rosa
Illustrator: Ruth Bennett/The Bright Agency
Series Advisor: Marjorie Frank

TABLE OF CONTENTS

There is a glossary on page 40. Terms defined in the glossary are in type **that looks like this** on their first appearance.

THE BOY CLIMBED THE TREE.

HE SAVED THE KITTEN.

This should work!

Whoa!

REEEOOW

Thanks, mister!

Hooray!

I want to help my daughter win the soccer game.

No problem.

Kid, hand me one of those **subjects!**

What's a subject?

The subject of the sentence is who, where, or what the sentence is about.

HORSES
EVERYBODY
CLEVELAND
THE GIRL
A FOX

PERIOD

Don't they teach you kids anything in school?

This one should do!

THE GIRL

What is the subject of the sentence
THE CAR DROVE DOWN THE STREET?
See page 40 for the answer.

PREDICATES

SENTENCE
DELIVERY & REPAIR!
Hurry!

PERIOD

Okay, now grab me one of those **predicates**.

Got it!

The predicate tells what the subject did... or something else about the subject.

SCORED A GOAL

WENT TO SCHOOL

RAN

WAS FUNNY

Here you go, ma'am.

THE GIRL SCORED A GOAL.

Later...

FRESH BANANAS

You see, most people don't know that there's more than one kind of sentence.

I specialize in **declarative sentences.**

SENTENCE DELIVERY & REPAIR

DOG TREATS

PER10D

There's one right now...

...and that's me at the end... a period!

HUNGRY KIDS LOVE APPLES.

SENTENCE DELIVERY & REPAIR

PERIOD

ORANGES ARE DELICIOUS.

THE CAT ATE THE TREAT.

GRANDPA READ THE BOOK.

UPSIDE DOWN

WE FIX CARS.

A declarative sentence states or declares a fact...

He likes to season his sentences with question words...

...to make **interrogative sentences.**

WHO

WHAT

WHERE

WHEN

WHY

Instead of declaring a fact...

An interrogative sentence <u>asks</u> for information.

PER1OD

What's your name, kid?

My name is **Comma.**

Did anybody ever tell you...

You look a lot like Period... with a little tail?

WHO becomes the subject of the sentence.

SOMEONE

WHO DRANK THE JUICE?

Don't forget the question mark!

Other times, you have to rearrange the order of the words...

THE MILK IS WHERE

...to bring the question word to the front.

This one is mine!

WHERE IS THE MILK

Find the question word in the sentence
WHY IS IT SO DARK?
See page 40 for the answer.

19

EXCLAMATORY SENTENCES

A few bites later...

DING

PERIOD

This looks important!

Let me see!

EXCLAMATION POINT

I need help!

Why didn't he just use a period?

This mark here is called an **exclamation point**.

It is used to mark an **exclamatory sentence**.

An exclamatory sentence expresses urgency or excitement.

The truck is on fire!

That's a good example.

No, I mean it!

That was a close one!

We should go see what my friend needs.

I came as fast as I could.

Come on in!

These sentences look weird!

① Call the building inspector.

② Look over the plans.

③ Pay the workers.

I can't find the subject.

Those are **imperative sentences**.

An imperative sentence tells someone what to do.

23

HANG THE LIGHTS.
FIX THE TOILET.
ORDER MORE NAILS.

As supervisor, it's my job to tell people what to do.

So, imperative sentences really come in handy.

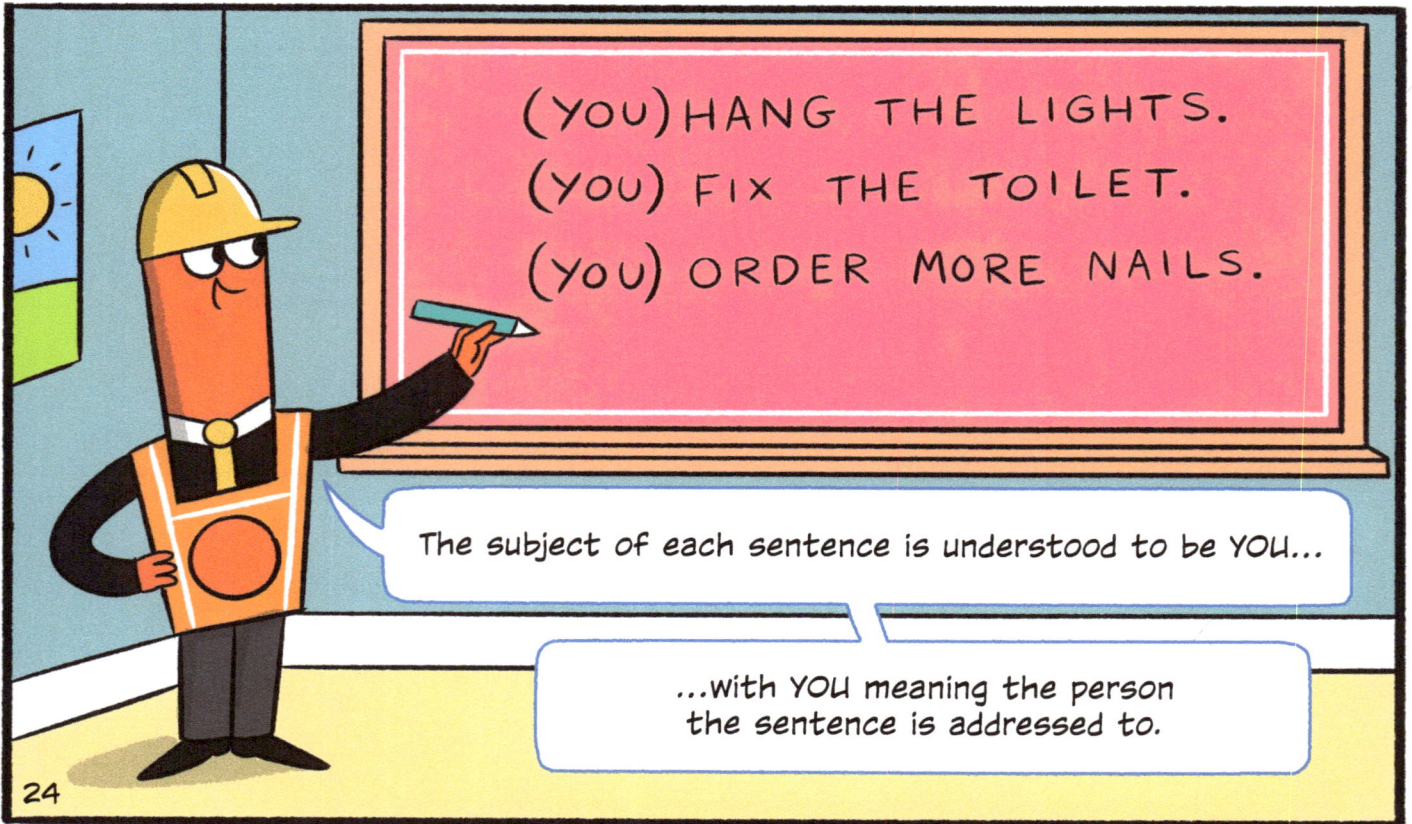

(YOU) HANG THE LIGHTS.
(YOU) FIX THE TOILET.
(YOU) ORDER MORE NAILS.

The subject of each sentence is understood to be YOU...

...with YOU meaning the person the sentence is addressed to.

Hold it steady.

Be careful!

I've noticed that some imperative sentences end in periods...

...and others end in exclamation points.

Mix the concrete carefully.

Usually, a period will do the job.

An exclamation point shows urgency or emotion.

Get this thing off my foot!

THUD

SORT THE SENTENCES

A huge shipment of sentences has arrived!
Help sort them into their proper types.

INTERROGATIVE SENTENCES

I AM READY TO GO!

WHIRRR

SUMMER IS TOO SHORT.

WHY DID YOU LEAVE?

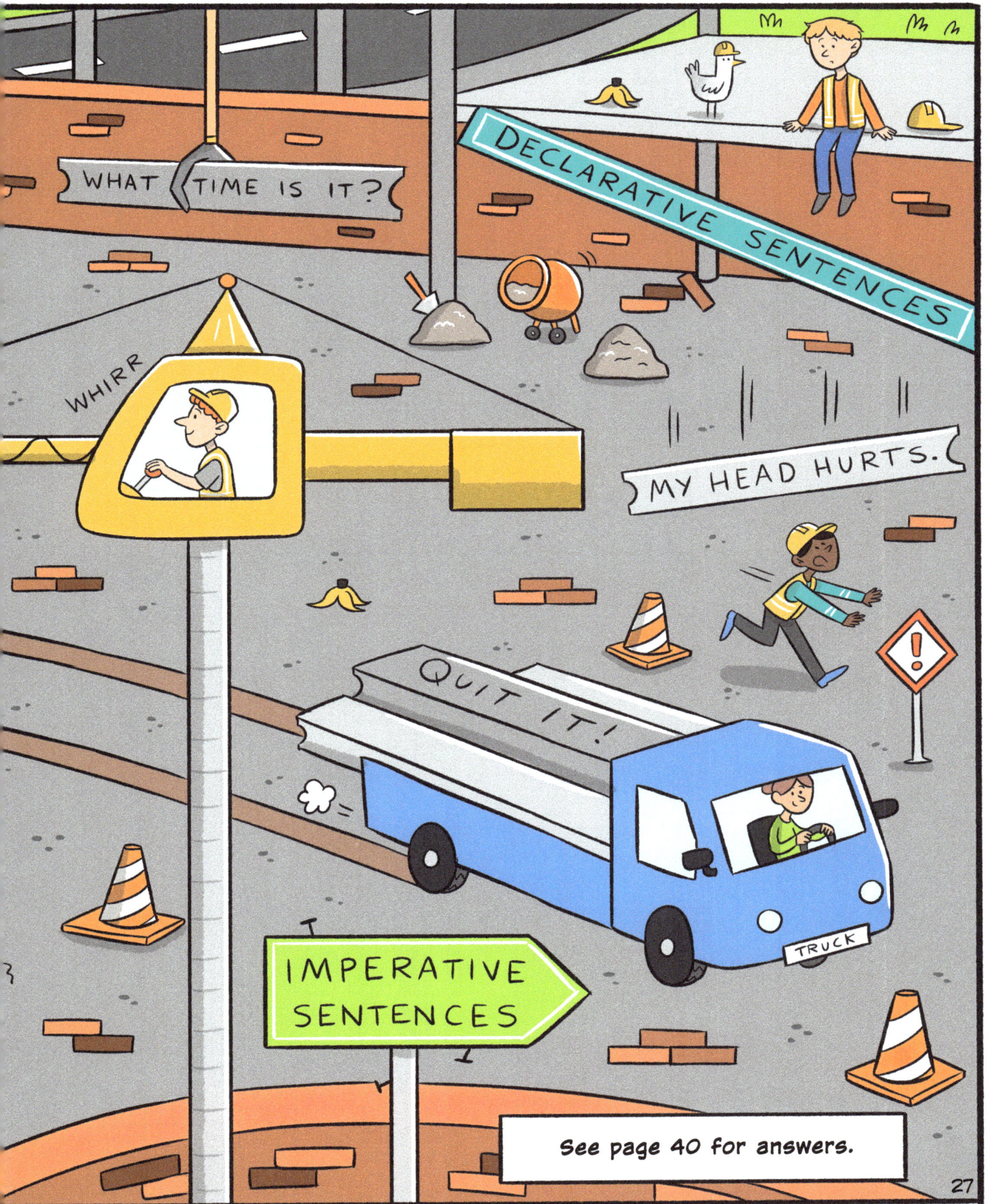

SENTENCE FRAGMENTS

Your message sounded urgent.

What do you need?

PERIOD

Some joker delivered to me all these **sentence fragments**.

A BIG DOG

WENT TO THE STORE

AFTER WORK

BOB'S TRUCK

RAN AWAY

DOWN THE STREET

I can't build with sentences that are incomplete.

Something's missing!

A BIG DOG

You got that right!

PERIOD

A complete sentence has a subject and a predicate.

COMPOUND SENTENCES

Here you go!

AUNT JENNY WENT TO THE STORE.

Good work!

PERIOD

Clean up the rest of these, kid...

...and Exclamation Point will give us a tour of the job site.

PERIOD

FLEW INTO THE SKY

THE BIRD

THE CAT

WAS DELICIOUS

THE PIE

SLEPT ON THE COUCH

Can you help Comma match the sentence fragments?
See page 40 for answers.

PERIOD

EAT YOUR DINNER OR GO TO BED EARLY.

THE TEACHER SPOKE AND THE STUDENTS LISTENED.

What are those long sentences up there?

Those are **compound sentences.**

THE SKY GREW CLOUDY

IT STARTED TO RAIN

A compound sentence includes two or more complete sentences that are closely connected.

The sentences are connected using a **conjunction...**

...a word such as AND, OR, or BUT.

THUD

BUZZZ

THE SKY GREW CLOUDY AND IT STARTED TO RAIN.

31

JULIE LOVED THE PLAY BUT CARLOS DID NOT

That should do it!

Good work, kid! How'd you do it?

PERIOD

As a comma, it's my job to make long sentences easier to manage.

ED THE PLAY BUT ...OS DID NOT LIKE

See! The comma helps separate the parts of a compound sentence...

...making it easier to read!

RUN-ON SENTENCES

My final lesson...

Always enjoy a break after a job well done.

CLINK

WHIRRRR

PERIOD

The workers started putting commas everywhere...

...just like you showed us.

HUFF

GROAN

CREAK

WOBBLE

But, something's gone terribly wrong!

I PLAYED BASKETBALL , MARVIN ATE DINNER.

You can't just put a comma anywhere!

This sentence doesn't even have a conjunction.

MARIA HELD THE BOOK AND GENE READ THE DIRECTIONS WHILE MOM COOKED

WOBBLE

WOBBLE

This sentence doesn't even have a comma.

It just goes on and on.

THE PAINTING WAS BEAUTIFUL AND IT HUNG IN A MUSEUM.

EAT YOUR DINNER, BRUSH YOUR TEETH.

This entire structure is riddled with **run-on sentences!** A run-on sentence improperly combines multiple different thoughts.

Um, can you help me clean this up?

That's the nice thing about the sentence business, kid...

There's always plenty of work to do!

A LITTLE FISH

GOT TO WORK ON TIME.

MY BIRTHDAY IS ON TUESDAY.

THE SUN WAS SHINING CLOUDS APPEARED.

MOM SANG, AND DAD PLAYED GUITAR.

I BROUGHT THE EGGS AND TINA BROUGHT THE BUTTER BUT PEDRO MIXED THEM TOGETHER.

Help sort the wreckage into complete sentences, run-on sentences, and fragments.
See page 40 for answers.

SHOW WHAT YOU KNOW

1. Identify the subject of each sentence.

A. Cleveland is a beautiful place.
B. The tree fell over.
C. Open the door.

2. Which punctuation mark or marks are used to end each type of sentence?

PERIOD

A. Declarative
B. Imperative
C. Interrogative
D. Exclamatory

3. FILL IN THE BLANKS

A. A _____ sentence includes two or more closely related ideas connected by a word called a _____.

B. Most sentences end with a _____.

4. Which of the following is a complete sentence?

A. FIVE DOLLARS.

B. THE BEAR ATE HONEY.

C. KEPT GOING AND GOING UNTIL IT WAS FAR AWAY.

See page 40 for answers.

ANSWERS

page 11: THE CAR

page 13: THE TEAM WON THE GAME.

page 19: <u>WHY</u> IS IT SO DARK?

page 27:

MOW THE YARD. -imperative
I AM READY TO GO! -exclamatory
SUMMER IS TOO SHORT. -declarative
WHY DID YOU LEAVE? -interrogative
WHAT TIME IS IT? -interrogative
MY HEAD HURTS. -declarative
QUIT IT! -imperative

page 29: AUNT JENNY

page 30:

THE BIRD I FLEW INTO THE SKY.
THE CAT I SLEPT ON THE COUCH.
THE PIE I WAS DELICIOUS.

page 37:

A LITTLE FISH -sentence fragment
MY BIRTHDAY IS ON TUESDAY. -complete
sentence
GOT TO WORK ON TIME. -sentence
fragment
THE SUN WAS SHINING CLOUDS
APPEARED. -run-on sentence

MOM SANG, AND DAD PLAYED GUITAR.
-complete sentence
I BROUGHT THE EGGS AND TINA BROUGHT
THE BUTTER BUT PEDRO MIXED THEM
TOGETHER. -run-on sentence

SHOW WHAT YOU KNOW ANSWERS
pages 38-39:

1. A. Cleveland
   B. The tree
   C. (You)

2. A. period
   B. period or exclamation point
   C. question mark
   D. exclamation point

3. A. A <u>**compound**</u> sentence includes two or more closely related ideas connected by a word called a <u>**conjunction.**</u>

   B. Most sentences end with a <u>**period.**</u>

4. B.

WORDS TO KNOW

comma (,) a punctuation mark used to separate parts of a sentence

compound sentence two or more simple sentences joined by a conjunction

conjunction a word such as and, or, or but that connects the two parts of a compound sentence

declarative sentence a sentence that states or declares a fact

exclamation point (!) a punctuation mark that indicates excitement or urgency

www.ingramcontent.com/pod-product-compliance
Lightning Source LLC
Chambersburg PA
CBHW060858090426
42737CB00023B/3488